Take a trip to
EGYPT

Keith Lye

General Editor

Henry Pluckrose

Franklin Watts

London   New York   Sydney   Toronto

Facts about Egypt

Area:
1,001,449 sq. km.
(386,683 sq. miles). This
is about twice the size of
France

Population:
45,414,000 (1983)

Capital:
Cairo

Largest cities:
Cairo, Alexandria,
El Giza

Official language:
Arabic

Main religion:
Islam

Major exports:
Cotton and cotton goods,
rice, fruit, vegetables

Currency:
Pound

Franklin Watts Limited
12a Golden Square
London W1

ISBN: UK Edition 0 86313 042 9
ISBN: US Edition 0 531 03758 4
Library of Congress Catalog Card No:
83-60902

© Franklin Watts Limited 1983

Text Editor: Brenda Williams
Maps: Tony Payne
Design: Peter Benoist
Photographs: Zefa; James Davis, 16, 17,
20, 26
Front and Back Covers: Zefa

Typeset by Ace Filmsetting Ltd,
Frome, Somerset
Printed in Hong Kong

Most of Egypt is hot desert. Its water comes from the River Nile. This great river is the world's longest and rises far away in the mountains of East Africa. Nine out of every ten Egyptians live in the Nile valley. The Nile valley was the home of one of the world's ancient civilizations.

For thousands of years, flat-bottomed boats called feluccas have carried people and goods up and down the River Nile. It is Egypt's only river. In the deserts, camels are the chief means of transport.

El Giza is near Cairo, Egypt's capital. At El Giza are the pyramids – the tombs of ancient Egyptian rulers called pharaohs. The pyramids remind us that Egypt had a great civilization 5,000 years ago.

The Great Sphinx at El Giza has
the head of a pharaoh and the body
of a lion. About a million people go to
Egypt every year to visit the sites and
treasures of ancient Egypt.

Abu Simbel in southern Egypt has two temples which are more than 3,200 years old. The ancient Egyptians had many gods and goddesses. They even thought that their pharaoh was a god.

This picture shows some stamps and money used in Egypt. The main unit of currency is the pound, which is divided into 100 piastres.

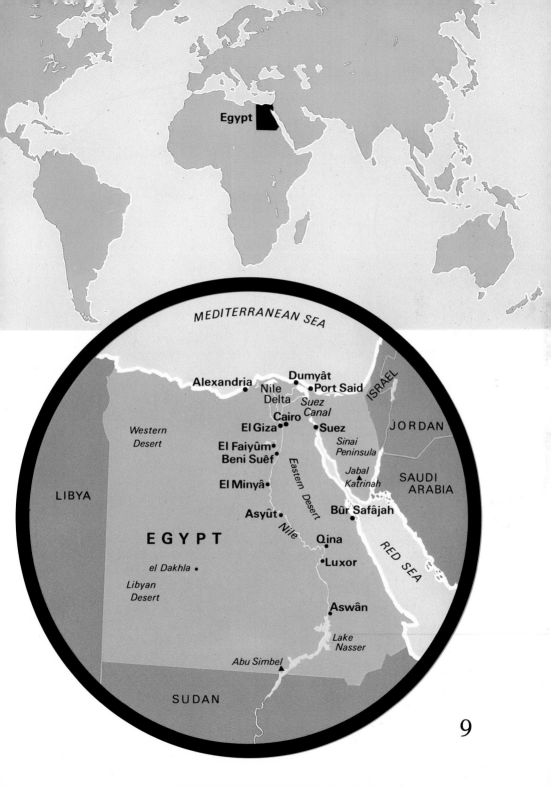

9

Treasures were placed in the tombs of the pharaohs. This golden throne was found in the tomb of King Tutankhamun. The people of ancient Egypt were great artists, architects, scientists and engineers.

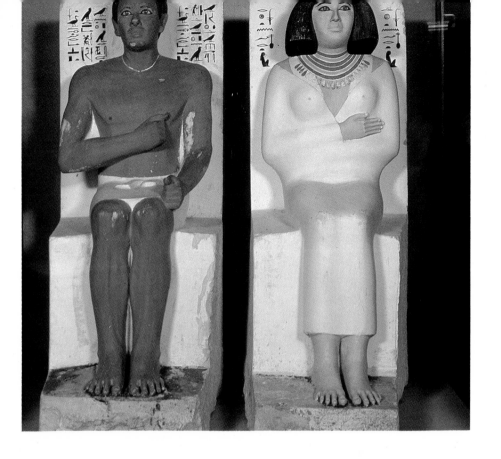

Prince Rahotep and Princess Nofert lived more than 4,000 years ago, in ancient Egypt's fourth dynasty. Dynasties are periods ruled by one royal family. Egypt had 31 dynasties between 3100 and 332 BC. In 332 BC, Alexander the Great conquered Egypt.

Cairo is the capital of the Arab Republic of Egypt, as the country is officially called. With over 8 million people, it is one of the world's largest cities. Most Egyptians are Arabs. Arabic is the official language.

Cairo has many old buildings and busy markets. Many Egyptians wear western clothes. But men and women also wear long, flowing robes called galabiyeh. Women once hid their faces behind veils. Few Egyptian women now do so.

The religion of Egypt is called Islam. Its followers are called Muslims. When Muslims pray, they face Mecca in Arabia, where the Prophet Muhammad was born. Muhammad founded Islam. He died in AD 632.

Behind this market in Cairo is a tower called a minaret. It is part of a mosque, where Muslims worship. A muezzin (crier) calls people to prayer from the top of the minaret.

Islam came to Egypt in AD 639–642. The Arabs built an empire that stretched from Spain to India. They also set up universities. Cairo's Al-Azhar University was built in 971.

16

Alexandria is Egypt's second largest city, with more than 2 million people. It is the leading port. It is on the Mediterranean Sea, near the Nile delta, a fertile area formed from river mud.

The Sultan Hassan Mosque in
Cairo is one of the city's most
beautiful buildings. The word Islam
means "submission" and Muslim
means "one who submits to God."

These children are learning about the Koran, the Holy Book which tells of the Prophet Muhammad's teachings. Although Islam is the main religion, some Egyptians are Coptic Christians.

A family enjoys a day's outing at Cairo Zoo. Family life in Egypt is much like that in western countries. Although Islamic law allows men to have four wives, most Egyptian men have only one wife.

Most Egyptian families enjoy watching television. Television arrived in 1960. By the late 1970s, more than a million homes in Egypt had television sets. Both foreign and Egyptian shows are broadcast.

Garlic, cloves, coriander and other spices are sold in Egyptian markets. Spices are used to make sauces to eat with meat. Beans made into a paste with cotton oil, salt and lemon juice form fool, the national dish.

The number of people in Egypt –
about 45 million – grows by more
than a million a year. Many people
want homes in such cities as Port
Said, and so house builders are
always busy.

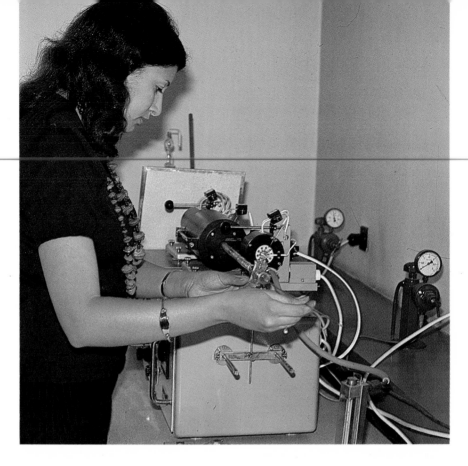

Egypt needs scientists if it is to raise the standards of living of its many poor people. Many girls study science. Egyptian women have more freedom than women in some other Arab countries, where they must stay at home.

Education in Egypt is free and all children from 6 to 12 years of age must go to school. This village class is at Dakhla Oasis in the Western Desert. More than half of adult Egyptians cannot read or write.

The High Dam at Aswan in southern Egypt holds back the River Nile and so prevents floods. Behind the dam is the man-made Lake Nasser. Its waters are used by farmers and to drive generators that make electricity.

Water is pumped from the Nile into irrigation channels, which carry it to the crops and date-palms. Irrigation made ancient Egypt a great civilization and is important today.

Animal-drawn ploughs and modern tractors are often seen side by side in Egypt. Farming employs about half of Egypt's workers. Peasant farmers are called fellahin. They grow various food crops but the most valuable crop and chief export is cotton.

The main iron and steel factories
in Egypt are at Helwan, near Cairo.
Egypt is North Africa's most
industrialized country, but only
about a third of its workers are
employed in industry. Other
industrial products are chemicals,
plastics and textiles.

Dakhla Oasis is surrounded by hot, sandy desert. But here water rises to the surface from underground rocks. Oases are green, fertile spots in the desert. Nomads visit oases so that their animals can drink.

The Suez Canal in Egypt links the
Mediterranean to the Red Sea. This
area was a battleground in Arab–
Israeli wars of 1956, 1967 and 1973.
But a treaty signed in 1979 has
brought peace to the canal region.

Index